finding love after 50

If you're single in this age of "everything connects," you absolutely need a virtual love hunter to guide you through the romance sites online. And if you're over 50 (admittedly 50 is the new 30) and shopping for a date, a partner, or a spouse, buy this book, consume it quickly, and start selling (profiles are everything) and browsing (you'll feel like a kid in an ice cream store). We all see experts in every aspect of our lives and here's one who can help you find love in this chapter of your life.

— **Marian Salzman**, trendspotter, author, and CEO, Havas PR North America

Cassie Keim is the perfect tour guide for an adventure on the "Romance Highway," her joyful metaphor for finding love when you're over 50. With nearly three decades of matchmaking experience, Cassie is a wise and loving friend, sitting on the passenger side, dispensing helpful advice and firmly, but gently, encouraging us to face our fears and enjoy the journey on our terms.

— **Patrice Tanaka**, Chief Joy Officer, Joyful Planet and author, *Becoming Ginger Rogers*, and co-author, *Beat the Curve*

finding love after 50

Modern Dating Strategies for Women
from an Industry Insider

CASSIE ZAMPA-KEIM

InnovativeMatch Publishing
SAN FRANCISCO

Author: Cassie Zampa-Keim
Writer: Danielle Machotka
Cover design, interior design by JM Shubin, Book Alchemist
(www.bookalchemist.net)

CATALOGING DATA:
Finding Love After 50:
Modern Dating Strategies for Women
from an Industry Insider
by Cassie Zampa-Keim

ISBN: 978-0-9964390-9-1

First Printing 2016
Printed in the United States of America

*For the women and men who have believed in me
and trusted my help on their journey down the
Romance Highway. Their courage to get out there
again is inspiring.*

contents

introduction

It's never too late to start a trip down the Romance Highway. The beauty of this particular road is that it allows you to take the dating journey *you* are seeking. Whether you are looking for companionship, a life partner, or something yet to be discovered, you can define your goals and move at the pace that is comfortable for you. There are many ways to get to where you want to be.

Finding Love After 50 will be your ultimate guide on this journey. Using my nearly three decades of experience in the dating industry and real-life examples of people just like you who have already traveled down this road, I will give you all the tools you need to find a partner who will add to your already rich life.

Dating can feel overwhelming at any age, but when you haven't done it for a while, even the question of where to start can stop you in your tracks. This book is designed to help you get rolling, map out a route, understand and navigate obstacles, and get to your destination in the shortest amount of time. Most importantly, *Finding Love After 50* puts this journey completely in your hands, rather than in the hands of an expensive matchmaker.

The matchmaking industry works well for many people. Matchmaking companies take on "attractive, educated, successful, nonsmoking" clients who pay anywhere from $10,000 to $200,000 for the service. A matchmaker works with the client, sending them matches they feel are suitable on a quota system (the company agrees to make a certain number of matches in a certain time period). In general, matchmakers send matches without including photos, and give the client feedback forms to evaluate how dates went. Women often sign up for matchmaking services feeling secure that they will be introduced to like-minded men who share a similar financial status and have the same commitment to finding a partner, based on the fact that the men also paid an equivalent sum of money to join the service.

Women under fifty often find success with this method. The reality for women over fifty, however, is very different. Most men in that age range who are dating simply do not sign up for matchmaking services, and the pool of available males should really be called a puddle. What's more, a small percentage of the men in the database in that demographic have actually paid for the service; the rest have been asked to join by matchmakers trying to even out the gender discrepancy in sign-ups, which sets up an uneven relationship between the women and men from the beginning. Of course, most services will not tell you that, leading you to believe that they have plenty of available and interested men in your demographic. I was in the matchmaking industry for many years before switching my focus to dating strategies for women and men over fifty, and I have seen firsthand how the matchmaking industry fails women in that age group. The good news is that you can do much more for yourself than the industry would do for you, at almost no cost and with a much greater rate of success. I have been doing it for clients for many years now, and I am going to show you how.

What about online dating? That probably was not around the last time you were looking for a life companion. Online dating can feel scary, too public, or just for the younger generation. It's not. Done properly, it opens up a world of people and possibilities that exponentially increase your chance of finding the person you want to be with at any age, for fun and adventure, for life, or for both. I believe that online dating is the best thing to come along for any age group, but especially for women over fifty. There is a ridiculously large pool of people to draw from, you get to be proactive and choose the profiles you are interested in, and the whole process is transparent, unlike with traditional matchmaking. Online dating has significantly improved the chances for women over fifty to find partners, and is easy to learn to use.

In 2008, after working in traditional matchmaking for almost two decades, I started looking at online dating sites, and what I found over two years of research was astounding. There were plenty of quality men over fifty on those sites. I realized that I could provide great options—and many of them—for clients, keeping my personal connection to them while helping them navigate online dating. My focus shifted from just matchmaking to coaching clients in dating strategies and helping them through the process. The online dating world and social networking sites have exponentially increased the number of people available to my clients, and I have become an expert at reading and understanding profiles (digital body language) and helping my clients find matches.

I have seen the evolution of the matchmaking industry and also witnessed the rise of online dating. As a result, I can confidently say that women over fifty have a terrific chance of finding the level of love or companionship they are seeking, simply by using the tools and ideas in this book.

Skeptical about finding love on your computer or phone? Author and relationship expert Dr. Christie Hartman says that online dating is the No. 1 way people fifty and over meet other singles.[1] My experience has borne that out, as well. Keep reading to find out how to navigate the online dating world to maximize your chances of meeting the right person for you, at a pace and in a way that is comfortable.

Finding a partner is not always easy or quick. As you no doubt remember, dating can be frustrating and discouraging at times. The reasons are universal: it seems like there are no good candidates out there, it takes too much energy, it feels like a waste of time, bad dates are no fun, life is too busy, and dating doesn't easily fit into your schedule. All of these reasons can feel real at any given time, but none of them is a reason to stop trying. As with anything worthwhile in life, there are setbacks to endure and learning to absorb. But the rewards in the end will outweigh the challenges.

This book is written for women in their fifties, sixties, and beyond. This is a rich stage in life. You know yourself better than you ever have. You have established a career, or raised a family, or traveled the world, or become an expert at something, or all of the above. Perhaps you have experienced great love and lost it. Perhaps you have not found love yet. Whatever the circumstance, you have had time to learn what works for you and what doesn't, what fulfills your life and what drains it, what sort of people you love to be around, and what sort you avoid. You have most likely spent time learning about yourself, recognizing strengths and weaknesses, and improving the things that don't work. In short, you have cut out many of the problems people in their twenties and thirties face when they are dating, simply by living your life. You are starting your next journey on the Romance Highway from a good place.

I come to this topic with a tremendous passion for working with women over fifty, a passion formed by my own history. In 1990 I was diagnosed with advanced cancer, an experience that helped me to learn firsthand the value of companionship and how basic and important the desire for human connection is. I was in college at the time and did not know that my career would take me where it has, but the reality of people's need for other people was cemented in my psyche. I experienced loss and a lack of control over life's circumstances at a very young age, giving me compassion for others who find themselves in situations of loss, such as divorce or widowhood.

My early career was spent working for a dating service when the matchmaking industry as it exists today had not yet started. I immediately was drawn to and felt tremendous respect for clients in their forties, fifties, and sixties who were struggling with loss, trying to figure out where they were in their lives and where they wanted to be, and who were eager to meet someone. Even though I had not yet lived their years, I had, in a different way, lived their experiences of loss and desire for companionship.

During almost twenty years in the industry, I saw again and again the pattern of women over fifty signing up for matchmaking services while men in the same demographic did not. I felt these women's frustration acutely, and felt powerless when the database was empty for them. That was when I started researching online dating. This book represents all that I've learned about finding love in the 21st century, online and off, since 2008.

I use the metaphor of the Romance Highway to emphasize that dating is not like a tunnel, with only one way through and no detours. Highways offer multiple routes, different speeds, off ramps, frontage roads, and rest stops. Your journey will be based on your life as it is today, and will not be exactly like anyone else's. My goal is to help you see who *you* are and what brings you joy, an awareness that will increase your confidence and magnetism. This book will start you on a journey of discovery, an exciting evolutionary process that brings a new level of self-knowledge, clarity, and ultimately, relationship success.

Excited? Great! Buckle up, pack appropriately, and let your trip down the Romance Highway begin.

---

[1] Dr. Christie Hartman, "Some Interesting Online Dating Statistics," blog on her website,
http://christiehartman.com/some-interesting-statistics-on-online-dating/.

1 let the fun begin!

a woman I'll call Amanda (all names have been changed to protect client privacy) came to me saying she really wanted to date and meet new people, but was not interested in a relationship. Recently divorced after twenty-six years of marriage, she felt she didn't need anybody long-term in her life; she preferred to meet people for drinks or dinner and leave it at that. I applauded her for her clarity and asked her what types of men she'd like to meet. Her list was straightforward and reasonable: college-educated, nonsmoker, a father, divorced or widowed, kind, trusting. It was also in many ways the antithesis of her ex-husband, who was emotionally unavailable, traveled a lot, and became less and less interested in her needs and desires. (Clearly she had figured out exactly what didn't work for her!)

Amanda's divorce had left her with an emotional wall that she wasn't about to let anyone scale. She was self-sufficient; she had her work, children, and friends, and she was convinced that was enough. I understood she didn't want to get hurt again, but what Amanda didn't realize was that she couldn't achieve a deep sense of happiness, or even contentment, without risking getting hurt, without letting herself be vulnerable.

I asked her what she did when she wasn't working. Her answer was simple: she was taking care of her children and that was it; she was not doing anything just for herself. I followed up with the question of what she had loved doing before marriage, family, and work took over her life, and discovered she enjoyed tennis and hiking. So I suggested that she start making time for both, slowly incorporating them into her daily routine. She found it hard to find the time in her busy life, but I convinced her that she had to discover ways to start feeling good about herself again, and in the process, create a bigger network for herself.

Amanda joined a tennis club, started playing on a team, and met several new people, including a few men she liked and went on dates with. After this step, I felt she was ready to start online dating. Although hesitant, she let me work with her to create and post a profile, and soon started hearing from interested men. After her first date she reported that the guy had been great, and that she enjoyed the process of meeting new people in this casual way. That one positive experience convinced her that online dating wasn't so bad. In fact, much to her surprise, she began to meet attractive, interesting men with whom she had a lot in common. The domino effect set in— which I see happen all the time in situations like this— and she started meeting great guy after great guy.

Three months into the process, I set Amanda up with a man I knew named Henry. She immediately felt attracted and connected to him, which she had never experienced on a first date. She wanted to see him again. Unfortunately, he didn't appear to feel the same way. Sometimes in situations like this, and with permission from my client, I will contact the date to get feedback. When I contacted Henry, he reported that Amanda had spent the date telling him how full her life was, how much she loved her life, and how she loved being independent. He was attracted to her, but it didn't seem that there was any room in her life for him or anyone else. I shared Henry's feedback with Amanda and pointed out that men want to feel that they fit into a woman's life, that they are not being squeezed into a space that is already too full. What Amanda didn't realize was that she had succeeded in building an impenetrable emotional wall, which blocked her from attracting someone she really liked.

I worked with Amanda on how to present herself to men on dates, and how to open up space for them in her life without losing sight of who she was. She worked on the things we discussed, and three months later she met someone with whom she is still involved.

The key to Amanda's success was her attitude. She merged onto the Romance Highway with a positive attitude, a willingness to try something new, and a lack of neediness. Once she added a willingness to let herself feel vulnerable, she came out in an even better place than she had expected.

new isn't always easy

Dating again after a long period of time might not be the easiest thing to do, but it should be fun. To some, that might seem impossible. Others, eager to get going, are looking forward to the excitement of meeting new people and broadening their social circles. Wherever you fall on the continuum between these two extremes, however, the bottom line is that dating truly can be fun. And the more you enjoy it, the better your chances of a successful outcome, whatever *successful* means in your life today—a long-term relationship, companionship, casual dates, or just more good friends.

People who have been through divorce or have been widowed often enter the dating world with insecurities about where to start, what to do, and whether they really measure up. We all age and change, and of course we do not look or feel like we did in our twenties or thirties. (Neither does anyone else out there in the dating world that you might be interested in!) The pain of losing a loved one through divorce or death can make us uncertain about investing emotionally again. Individuals who have never been married but have dated for a long time often suffer uncertainty as well, feeling frustrated that there is no one out there who is right for them. None of these things make dating sound like fun.

Some shifts in thinking and a little groundwork, however, can go a long way toward alleviating those doubts, and give dating a new and invigorating shine.

embrace a fresh perspective

The first step is to go into dating with the right attitude, as Amanda did. Creating the right mindset is critical before you start this new phase of your life. If you fear dating and assume that it won't work for you, your results will reflect that. If you go into it with an open mind, a strong sense of who you are and what you are looking for, and patience for the process, you are much more likely to attract and find people you enjoy spending time with.

Motivational speaker, self-help author, and life coach Tony Robbins recommends adopting a transformational vocabulary to change the quality of your life.[1] As he says, "Words you habitually choose also affect what you experience... [T]he words that we attach to our experience become our experience, regardless of whether it's objectively accurate or not."

For example, instead of saying, "I'm old and men only date younger women," you could say to yourself, "I am a beautiful woman and would make a great partner." You might not change what happens around you (although, in fact, you might), but you will change how you perceive what happens and how you react to it, and in the process, you will create a more positive atmosphere for yourself and those around you.

identifying who you are and what you want in a partner

A widow named Kate had had zero luck with online dating sites and after a year had come to the conclusion that there were no good men out there looking for serious relationships. After about a half-hour of talking to Kate about the men she was finding online and dating, it became obvious that she was repeating the same mistake over and over. She was drawn only to business executives who had gone to good schools, since they represented the high-status world in which she wanted to circulate. What she found is that these men were for the most part emotionally unavailable, were interested in much younger women, and were generally not looking for long-term relationships. Thinking she could change their minds, she continued to seek out the same type. But nothing ever changed, and she became frustrated and disillusioned with her prospects.

Kate's experience illustrates why I have my clients go through a series of questions to clarify where they are in their lives *before* they start dating. As people re-enter the dating world, they often have a hard time either knowing or accepting what their lives are today. If they bury the reality of their lives, they end up with the wrong people. If they can accept where and who they are, they can identify what truly matters to them, and who will really work for them in a relationship. By taking a closer look at their lives, criteria that might have seemed critical become less important, and criteria they might have ignored often move to the top of the list. Kate thought that dating someone who had gone to a good school was a high priority. Instead, it turned out that interest in a long-term, grounded relationship was more important to her in a man.

I have compiled a list of questions that will help you look at yourself and your life very honestly, taking stock of the good and the bad, to create a solid place from which to start dating. To do this exercise effectively, write down your answers, don't just go over them in your head. Writing things down is not only therapeutic, it also helps you clarify your thoughts and absorb the answers more completely.

In this process you will look at your life and see where you are and what you need and want. I can't say it enough: knowing yourself is critical. Start by asking, "Would I date myself?" If the answer is no, look at why that is. You need to go into the dating process feeling good about yourself, and accepting what you are and are not. Here you actually have an advantage over people in their twenties and thirties, as you have had time to get to know yourself and are clearer about who you are and whom you want in your life.

For some people, the reason they would not date themselves has to do with appearance. Others recognize personality traits that can be challenging. None of these things will change overnight, but if you recognize a potential challenge to attracting others, you can start to work on it. Begin an exercise program, even if you have to start off slowly. Change your eating habits little by little. Buy some new clothes or try a new hairstyle. Ask your friends to be honest with you about personality traits, and think about how you might work on them. Above all, find peace with who you ultimately are and don't try to change yourself into someone you are not. Your goal is to bring your honest self to the table, in life as well as in dating.

Next, note all your best qualities. Read the list over, absorb it, and use it occasionally to remind yourself of all the good things you have to offer. Write down the things you would like to change, and use that list as a motivator. Don't consult it too often and don't let it discourage you, but use it as a reminder of the ways in which you would like to change.

Once you have considered all these factors, ask yourself what type of relationship would best fit your life right now? Are you looking for a companion for outings, activities, and travel? A spouse? Or are you looking for more than one person to spend time with casually? Are you interested in physical intimacy? Your feelings about any of these things might change as you get deeper into dating, but it is important to go into your journey with knowledge of how you feel today about what would work best for you.

A final, critical step is to acknowledge what has and hasn't worked for you in past relationships. Think of your most recent one to three significant relationships and make a list of the positives and negatives of those relationships. Try to remove any residual anger and look at the relationships with the benefit of distance and a healthy dose of honesty. You don't want to keep repeating the same mistakes and ending up with the same type of person that hasn't worked for you in the past. In addition, look at what your former partners have said about the relationships and see if there is anything you can take away from that.

Look at your list whenever you are feeling uncertain about someone or sensing that you are repeating a familiar pattern. Give yourself permission *not* to repeat that pattern in your future relationships.

You might find, as you start to date and meet new people, that certain things change in your answers to these relationship questions. In addition, as you become increasingly sure of yourself in the dating world, your confidence will grow, and you'll be able to add more positive items to your list. At the same time, the type of relationship you are looking for might change, perhaps morphing from companion to lover or from lover to marriage. Anything is possible as you discover your place in the world of dating.

As for Kate, after answering the questions she began to change her perception of what she was looking for and what her priorities for a relationship were. In the end, she met a successful attorney who had, as it turns out, gone to a good school but did not need to move in high-society circles. Her new partner was down-to-earth, supportive, kind, generous, and looking for a committed relationship. He is now committed to her, and she has moved across the country to be with him. When she became focused on the priorities that really would work for her, she found someone with the attributes that made her feel grounded and peaceful, without settling for less than she wanted.

Questions to help you identify the right person for you today

1. Would I date myself? If so, why? If no, why not?

2. What are my best qualities?

3. What would I like to change about myself?

4. What kind of relationship am I looking for right now? Casual dates? A companion? A lover? A spouse?

5. What has worked for me in my past one to three significant relationships? What has not worked in those relationships, and why?

6. What did my partners say to me about the relationships and what can I learn from that?

see the dating myths for what they are: myths

Perhaps the biggest myth about dating is that there are no good people out there. Here's the good, myth-busting news: There are. Lots of them. In the 2010 U.S. Census, there were 26.9 million singles in the United States aged fifty-five and older. Even if many of them are not looking for love or are not in the right demographic or geographic range, the numbers are still favorable. And with a pool like that, there are guaranteed to be plenty of people who could fit your life today.

Another myth is that unmarried men, especially those in their fifties or sixties, will never get married. I have seen many men in this age group find real love and happily move into marriage. If marriage is what you are after, don't be discouraged by meeting men who have never been married. There are often good reasons why, and there is always the chance that you will be the one they realize they want to be with. While sometimes it is true that men who have never tied the knot are selfish or set in their ways, you can always broach the fact that someone has never been married before you get too involved, and listen closely to what he has to say. You never have to commit yourself if someone doesn't seem serious about or capable of a long-term relationship.

Online dating has spawned its own set of myths. One is that men who post profiles are married, cruising (having fun and seeing what's out there, interested in meeting many women, and not yet committed to the process of finding a partner), or just looking for hookups. While there are people who fit these categories, it is usually evident from their profiles, and you can avoid those men fairly easily just by looking for a few red flags. I'll describe how to read digital body language in Chapter 3.

A common belief about online profiles is that everyone misrepresents themselves. It is true that men sometimes are a bit hazy about their age, height, hair, and income, and women about their age and weight. But if physical and financial attributes are what concern you most, it's likely you'll find it hard to meet the right person for reasons other than that someone fudged the numbers on his profile page. Focus too strongly on one physical trait or the size of a man's portfolio and you risk missing out on a world of wonderful (and suitable) people.

tame your fears

Fear is a natural part of starting anything new. We can think of a million things that could go wrong, and once those thoughts take over, we stall, procrastinate, and often get completely stuck. Dating involves emotional risk, just as all relationships do. But also just like any good relationship, the potential rewards are more than worth the emotional risks.

In a *Harvard Business Review* article, leadership coach Peter Bregman says that taking risks is the unexpected antidote to procrastination.[2] Watching surfers off a beach in Malibu one morning, he realized that every single ride ended the same way: the surfer fell into the water. Whether she was knocked off by the wave or rode it to the end, the outcome was always the same. Which got him thinking: "What if we all lived life like a surfer on a wave?" If we did, he concluded, we'd take more risks.

Bregman contends that the reason we don't do so is that we are afraid of feeling. Feeling rejected, feeling disappointed, feeling inadequate, feeling like a failure, feeling anything unpleasant. But as he says, "Our fear doesn't help us avoid the feelings; it simply subjects us to them for an agonizingly long time." So we need to get over our fears and start taking risks to open up to the wonderful possibilities in life.

How do we do that? Practice! As Bregman notes, there is no way to get better at taking risks other than to simply take them. Allow yourself to feel all the emotions that come up while you are taking that risk, breathe deeply, and keep doing it. Eventually you'll find that the downside is not as bad as it seems, and the upside is fantastic.

I appreciate that dating involves taking a chance and being vulnerable. I also appreciate that both can be frightening. That's why I always ask my clients what is more important: hiding behind the fear because it feels easier in the short run, or sticking their neck out and knowing the rewards can be amazing? Don't let fear drive you. Gather confidence from the fact that you have made it through loss in the past and that you are now okay. Have faith that you can do this again. And that you will be okay again.

As the saying goes, you must make a choice to take a chance or your life will never change.

live for the process, not the outcome

By starting to date, you are acknowledging that you would like to meet someone special. That is the highly desired, potentially life-altering outcome. But getting to that outcome involves a process, and if you don't enjoy the process, you are less likely to achieve your hoped-for results.

What does enjoying the process look like? Opening yourself up to the growth and expansion that dating can offer. Being excited about the potential to meet new people, ones you would have never met otherwise. Broadening your social circle. Learning about yourself. Growing in unexpected ways. Exposing yourself to new worlds through the people you meet and the process of dating. Letting go of the pressure to find "The One," or the sense that you have no idea how to date. Convincing yourself that this will be fun, whatever the end result.

If you find yourself thinking that you could never imagine enjoying dating, take small steps to change your mindset. Focus on just one area listed above—self-growth, for instance—and visualize its positive aspects. Then choose another—perhaps meeting new people and broadening your social circle. You might not see it all as positive at once, and you might slip back into negative thoughts and feelings about the whole process, but give yourself a chance to change your thinking and it will come.

transitioning from thinking to doing

So how do you get going? Laying some groundwork for the process is easier than it seems. Here are four steps to help you move from thought to action.

Nurture your Personal Tree of Life

Have you ever noticed how certain people seem to radiate happiness and attract others? This is because positive people attract other positive people. To start the dating process, you want to find a more positive outlook, which starts with nurturing your own Personal Tree of Life.

What is the Personal Tree of Life? Its roots are the foundation of your life. They started in childhood and have grown and created a solid foundation for you over the course of your life as you have grown. The trunk is your core, from which emanate the branches of your life experience—people and events that have shaped who you are today. You have to take good care of your Personal Tree of Life to keep it healthy and thriving. Eat right, exercise, practice positive affirmations, surround yourself with life-enhancing people. Feel rooted in the decisions you make. Trust that where you are in life is where you are supposed to be right now. You need your tree to keep you grounded and solid, especially when you start dating. That stable base will help you feel good about yourself and give off an attitude that attracts men and allows for solid relationships.

Dating is often a mirror of our lives. When we have low self-esteem, we unconsciously enter relationships with people who also do not value us. It's critical to find ways to view yourself positively, and to slowly build a solid, positive self-image. When you do, you will find that the mirror effect works wildly in your favor. You will begin attracting people who recognize what you bring to a relationship and who value you for it.

Maintain positive thinking

The first step to dating is feeling good. Re-read the positive traits you wrote about in the list of questions I gave you. If you haven't already, post them somewhere where you can easily see them. This will help you manage self-doubt by accepting who you are today. It's important to honor yourself in the present so you can get yourself moving—mentally and physically—in the right direction.

The more you can focus on what's good in your life, what you *do* have rather than what you *don't*, the better you will feel about your life overall. The more you do this, the more automatic it will become to be positive and optimistic—about your life, about yourself, and about dating.

The next time you find yourself thinking anything negative about dating, remind yourself not to let self-doubt and fear hold you back. Set the stage and put your life in motion.

Move forward, even in small steps

Dating is a methodical process. Think about your comfort level and assess your fears. Don't jump too fast or force yourself into anything. If you are a widow or divorcee, it's important to remind yourself that you've already been through hard times and that you can do this.

Take active steps. You won't find a new partner or friend by sitting around the house. Think of activities you would enjoy doing with a partner, and write them down. Next, do some of them on your own. This will help motivate you to be active and move away from the feeling that your life is on pause.

Explore online dating websites. If you feel uncomfortable or are worried about an ex seeing you online, make the choice to start off small. You don't have to post a profile picture. You can still interact with others and begin to familiarize yourself with online dating practices.

Starting small can also mean visiting smaller dating sites. Large communities like Match.com and eHarmony can be unnerving. Instead, try choosing a small dating website that isn't as crowded or intimidating. Some of these sites are better for finding a partner who shares your common interests and values. Websites like JDate.com, ChristianMingle. com, and RightStuffDating.com are good sites to look into. As noted earlier, Chapter 3 will delve into the online dating world in greater detail.

Expand your network

Making new friends and opening yourself up to new relationships is not easy. But a wider circle of activities and people in your life means more chances of meeting someone special at any given time.

Use new activities (or ones you used to love and are picking up again) as an opportunity to meet people. Pursuing interests will put you back in the people arena. Making new friends and expanding your social network will give you a new support system and increase your self-confidence. Remember Amanda at the beginning of the chapter?

After divorce, many people experience the splitting up of extended family and friends. New friends offer new perspectives—they know you for who you are now, and don't carry the weight of anything in your past. They can give you a newfound confidence to get out into the world, and might even offer great advice.

Once you have laid the groundwork, you are ready to start dating—and enjoying it! But dating now isn't like it used to be, and it's important to understand the changes. Chapter 2 will discuss what is new since the last time you were looking for love.

1 Tony Robbins, "The Power of Words: Transform Your Vocabulary, Transform Your Life!" The Anthony Robbins Blog, https://training.tonyrobbins.com/the-power-of-words-transform-your-vocabulary-transform-your-life/.

2 Peter Bregman, "The Unexpected Antidote to Procrastination," Harvard Business Review, May 10, 2013, https://hbr.org/2013/05/the-unexpected-antidote-to-pro/.

2 dating with confidence in the 21st century

J ulie and her husband grew apart after thirty-eight years of marriage, and divorced. Julie was interested in dating again, but was intensely uncomfortable about meeting people online. She didn't want friends to see her online, felt online dating wasn't organic—a phrase I hear over and over from clients—and told me that it didn't feel safe. She was still working and most of her friends were still married. Her pool of prospects was small.

This is a scenario I see repeated almost daily with my clients. Most of us who are or were married met our spouses "the old-fashioned way." We were introduced by friends, we met through work, we met through a shared activity or church group, or any number of other ways we happened to cross paths.

In the early years of adulthood, things are often quite fluid for us. Very little ties us down, and we feel free to change anything that is not working—job, dwelling, friends, the city we live in. In that free and untethered world, the possibilities are endless, and the number of people we meet seems to be, too.

As we get older, that changes. We get more settled in careers and jobs, we have children, we buy a house, our circle of close friends shrinks to those with whom we truly have things in common, and we align ourselves with communities of like-minded people. While our lives get richer and more mean-ingful, our circles in many ways get smaller. This is where Julie found herself after her divorce.

Dating in the 21st century feels very different than it did last century, and it is. Technology has infiltrated our lives in so many ways, including dating; communication modes have changed; the ex-pectations for dates have changed; and more women have bigger roles in the workforce.

But it's not only the dating world that is different. You are different now than you were in your twenties and thirties, and that plays a big role in under-standing what dating can be for you today, and how you can be successful at it. Confidence is so important in finding a partner, and part of that confidence comes from knowing and owning (and even loving) who you are today. It also comes from having a voice and knowing how and when to use it. You might not be there yet, but that is okay. This book will help you develop both confidence and your voice if you—like so many women—need to rediscover both.

what's changed in the dating world— the role of technology

Our world has gone tech. It's increasingly rare to get through the day without using a computer or mobile phone. Not surprisingly, dating has moved online, as well. What might be surprising is that online dating has been around for long enough now (over twenty years!) that it has become quite sophisticated. You now have a lot of control over the process and how you go about finding a partner online.

The Pew Research Center found that Americans' attitudes towards online dating shifted significantly over an eight-year period starting in 2005, when it first began studying online dating habits. In 2005, 44 percent of respondents felt that online dating was a good way to meet people. By 2013 that number had grown to 59 percent.[1] Not everyone meets "The One" online, and not everyone ends up even going on a date from their online experience, but in your fifties and beyond, it is a terrific way to broaden your circle and meet people who are local but whom you might not otherwise come into contact with. It's even likely that someone you meet online will know someone you already know.

If you are apprehensive about online dating, ease into it slowly. Chapter 3 will discuss online dating in much more depth, as well as suggest ways to dip your toes into the water. No matter how quickly you embrace online dating, however, it is important to go into it with the attitude that you have nothing to lose and everything to gain.

softening the impact of technology

We have to accept technology's role in our lives, but even if we don't love its many facets, we can adapt them to our own preferences. It is very easy today to hide behind the faceless modes of email and text communications. One of the things you do have control over in online dating is how you choose to communicate and how you get to know someone. An online dating site might provide the introduction, but it is up to you to take it from there—and to take technology out of the picture when it comes to building a relationship. If a man only wants to communicate via email or texts, it's likely he isn't going to offer much in the way of emotional connection. You can tell a lot from a phone conversation—the person's tone and attitude, his level of interest, and his ability to communicate, among other things. It's a first opportunity to get to know him.

Be sure to have a conversation on the phone before you make a date with someone new. That conversation will go a long way toward forming a first impression. (And remember, it works the other way, too—it's also your chance to make a good first impression.) If you decide to move forward with a first date, try for something easy and low-key.

new rules for first dates

Yes, even the rules for first dates have changed. Remember going on double dates with friends who set you up with someone they were sure was perfect for you? It was usually dinner, which seemed to stretch on endlessly when you realized that the blind date was not such a good match after all, and your friends, thinking it was all going great, ordered another bottle of wine. Or going out to a bar with friends and getting stuck in a conversation with someone you were not that interested in? The good news is that you are in charge now and first dates don't have to be excruciating if you set them up to be light, breezy, and quick. Just a chance to get to know someone a little better.

Plan to meet for a glass of wine or a cup of coffee. Or take that cup of coffee and go for a walk in an open and public area. Schedule something that gives you a chance to talk, but doesn't commit you to hours together. That will come later if you both decide it feels right. Meet somewhere you feel comfortable and happy, somewhere pleasant, and set it up to be brief (but not speed-dating brief—give the guy a bit of your time).

Know that you are not expected to start an acquaintance with a man with something formal like a meal or movie anymore. And remember that you are in control of this process; you can set it up in whatever way is comfortable for you. It's likely the other person is feeling hesitant as well, so keeping it light and short the first time you meet will suit him, too.

women in the workforce

The number of women in the workforce continues to increase. While this is a positive thing, it has also changed some aspects of dating. If you were working when you met your first husband or life partner and continued to work, your career has likely advanced and you are in a position of greater power at work than you used to be. If you were forced to go back to work after divorce or widowhood, you have developed a new side of yourself within your profession.

Women's increased presence in the workforce has empowered them to be stronger and more assertive, traits that are critical in the workplace. But just as women are not interested in a man running their relationship as he might run his company, men are often not attracted to the harder-edge behavior that women have to exhibit to be successful in the workplace. Knowing when to put that edge away and adopt a softer and more feminine style is very important to dating success.

This can be hard when you go straight from work to a date. Work is stressful and nonstop, and you probably leave the office with lots of work issues still on your mind. You might have a long commute or sit in heavy traffic every day, stressors in their own right. Showing a vulnerable side and letting down your guard are not usually ways you act at work, and might be the furthest from how you feel when you leave the office. But on a date, those are traits that men tend to be most attracted to.[2] So remember when you leave the office to leave your office persona behind. Give yourself at least a half-hour to de-compress before you meet someone for the first time. When you are on a date, it's you he'll want to get to know, not the person you need to be at work.

the biggest change of all—you

Sometimes it is hard to take an honest look at ourselves and assess where and who we are today. We get caught up in thinking of ourselves as we were at some other time in our lives—a time that might have defined us for a while, but a time that has passed. There are many ways we get stuck in an old image of ourselves, and when we are stuck there, we will be less successful at dating. Why? Because we are selling ourselves as someone we are not, and we are looking for something that no longer fits our lives today.

There are many ways we do this. The first is physical. I will be the last person to deny anyone their anti-aging treatments, but remember: such methods are only about the surface. Your body is aging in other ways, and your energy and interests are probably changing as a result. You may feel as energetic as you ever have, but today your energy might be for hiking or travel rather than dancing all night in a club.

Emotionally, you are also not twenty anymore. You have lived too many rich experiences—and grown through them. You don't want the same things you wanted when you were a young adult (or at least I hope you don't). It is so important when you start the dating process not to run away from who you are today or try to sell yourself as the person you were yesterday. You want to meet a like-minded man who is truly compatible with you. Pretending you are something you are not will stand in the way of that. Not to mention that accepting and loving yourself for who you are now will give you a confidence that men will find hard to resist.

Whether you embrace change, deny it, or are accepting it slowly (it is, after all, inevitable), seeing yourself for who you are today, and seeing your lifestyle for what it is today, will help you meet someone who both fits into your life and enriches it.

Two women come to mind. Susan called me when she was forty-six, saying she wanted to find a partner and have a baby. She was ready to adopt or do whatever else it took to become a mother. She had been single for a long time and had built her life around her friends and her career as the CEO of a clothing company. Because she was so busy and traveled for part of every month, she planned to hire a nanny to take care of her baby. What she didn't realize is that most men in their late forties and early fifties (the ages I would recommend for her) already have children or have raised children, and are not as likely to want to start again with diapers and midnight feedings. They are looking for someone who can more easily fit into where *they* are today. While I believed that it was possible she could meet someone who wanted to have a child with her, I asked her to be open-minded and consider the possibility that meeting a man with children might be a more successful route to take.

Holly also wanted children, but at age forty-seven she had accepted that she wasn't going to have her own. Instead, she told me she wanted to meet a man with kids. This acceptance of where she was in her life and awareness of her options gave her a much better chance of success in the dating world.

I try not to tell my clients that they can't have what they say they want, but instead guide them through the process of discovering what will work best in their lives. With Susan, doing that led to her changing her priority from having a child herself to finding a man who had some already. As it turns out, she met a man with three children in grammar school, which she really enjoyed. Rather than needing to have her own child, she discovered that what she really wanted was to be part of a family.

An exercise I like to give my clients is to have them write down what their daily and weekly schedules look like: how much they work, what they do outside of work, what activities they prioritize, and how much time they feel they have to give to dating right now. I have them look at their list realistically and think about what type of partner would fit with where their lives are today: someone with a similar schedule, someone who enjoys the same activities, a parent (or not), someone athletic, someone involved in the community, someone committed to their religion. Sometimes they find that what they thought they wanted and what really works for them are two very different things.

It's all about lifestyle, lifestyle, lifestyle.

Compatibility requires finding the people whose lifestyles can merge with yours without one of you making too many sacrifices. You might feel you want to recreate a previous long-term relationship. But that relationship and that lifestyle developed organically over time, based on whatever was going on in both your lives. Things are different today—you are different today—and your relationships will be, too.

I had a client named Michael who was in his late forties. He had a very successful career and an amicable divorce behind him; he and his ex-wife were friends and helped each other out with the kids, who were mostly grown. This arrangement allowed him to be flexible and indulge his love of travel.

Michael told me he wanted to meet an independent woman in her late thirties who, like him, had a flexible schedule and older kids. I responded that the likelihood of finding a woman that age who fit those criteria was slim. Many women in that age group have much younger kids and jobs, and few are anything but flexible in their schedules. Their lifestyle was probably not going to be compatible with his.

I usually advise dating no more than five years older or younger, and recommended this to Michael, based on his strong desire to find someone who could travel with him. At first he could not see himself with someone closer to his age, but he eventually met someone four years younger who has a flexible career and children the same age as his, and they are happily dating and traveling.

building the confidence you need to start dating

Confidence is an internal trait, even if it does manifest externally. The confidence to start and navigate the dating process comes from a knowledge of who you are today, what *your* needs are (it's time to stop prioritizing the needs of those around you at the expense of your own), and whom you should be with in order to meet those needs. It also involves taking good care of yourself so that your body and mind align to exude an irresistible magnetism. Here are a few things you can do to build your confidence.

Practice daily positive affirmations
Okay, so this probably sounds a bit woo-woo, but the truth is—and there is scientific data to back this up—that the more you say and think positively about yourself, the more you will start to believe it and project confidence. Your affirmations don't have to be off-the-charts in their scope. Think of something basic that you can take in, like "I believe in myself" or "I am the best I can be."

Exercise and eat well

This might not look like a guaranteed confidence-booster, but if you are exercising regularly and eating foods that nourish your body, you will feel better both physically and mentally. Add the fact that you'll look better, too, and the confidence will flow.

Spend time with people who make you feel good

We all know the type—the people we have lunch with who affect us so positively we spend the rest of the afternoon feeling great about our lives. There are people in the world who make us feel good and there are those who bring us down. It's often not a question of good or bad, just different approaches to life. But who wants to feel bad? Seek out people who make you feel good and avoid those who make you feel like you're carrying around a ball and chain.

Invest in your appearance

This will be more important for some people than others, but sometimes making a change in your hairstyle, buying new makeup, or splurging on new clothes (date clothes?) will perk up your confidence. Sometimes a new outfit or a great new 'do is a nice boost.

finding your voice

Beyond feeling good mentally and physically, confidence also includes having a voice. We often lose both our confidence and our voice after divorce or widowhood. Sometimes our childhoods were such that we never developed a voice, and our marriages and other significant relationships might have reaffirmed that. But it's never too late to find or rediscover your confidence and your voice, and doing so will set up a much more successful, meaningful, and fun dating journey.

There are really two voices I'm talking about here. One is inside you, and it tells you how you are feeling about things, when you should pay attention, and when or why you are hesitant. It's important to listen to that voice; it comes from a deep part of you that probably knows you better than anyone, and its job is to take care of you.

Then there is the voice you project in the world. You might even have a few of them: your mom voice, your work voice, your friend voice. They all come from your basic personality but are modulated to fit the needs of each particular communication.

Your dating voice is a little different. When you have a solid dating voice, you are able to say what you want or need, without roaring like a lion or accusing your date of wrongdoing. Your effective dating voice uses phrases such as, "I would like..." "I want..." or "I am feeling...," rather than "When you do this..." or "You make me feel like..." For instance, if your date only communicates by text and that drives you crazy, you can say, "I would really like to hear your voice over the phone instead of just texting." You will find out how much he cares by his response to you using your voice. If he ignores or belittles your request, you know he's not the man for you. And how much better to find out early in the dating process than further down the road.

If the thought of talking like that makes you break out in a cold sweat, imagine small ways you can practice using your voice with others, and practice them. Expressing your needs is critical in any relationship. But if it feels too daunting to assert yourself with a man you are dating, then start with a good friend or family member, and see what happens. Not every interaction will change things in your favor, but more will start to fall in that direction if you practice than if you don't.

I had a client named Teresa who was a doctor with three grown children. She had been married for thirty-two years and divorced for a year. While she had a busy schedule, she had decided to make time for dating. She was happily seeing a man, except for one thing: they only met when it worked in *his* schedule. He was fun to be with when they did go out and Teresa hoped for a deeper relationship, but she began to get frustrated that he was seemingly never available at times that worked best for her. I told her she needed to be honest and let him know she wanted to meet when it was good for her as well. When she did so, he told her that he didn't really feel that committed to her and didn't see their relationship as long-term. Of course, he had been saying exactly that with his rigid schedule, but it took her being direct with him for him to be direct with her. If Teresa hadn't spoken up, she would have gone on dating him for much longer before discovering how he felt, and ended up frustrated that she had wasted her time.

Even though the outcome in this case wasn't a happy one, at least not initially, in the long run it was far better and healthier for Teresa to have used her voice and expressed her wishes. Gaining this voice has given her so much more confidence in the dating world. She now uses the metaphor of a warrior to describe how she feels—a warrior for her self-worth and how she wants to be treated. Awakening her inner warrior (I will talk more about this in Chapter 5) has meant she can avoid both going into major battle and getting trampled in her relationships with men.

the more things change...

The dating world is different than it used to be, and you are different than you used to be. Change can be challenging, intimidating, and even scary. But we know that change is inevitable, and the sooner we accept it—and even embrace it—the better off we'll be, whether in dating or any other part of life.

Fortunately, some things never change. Despite the prevalence of technology, people still want human connection. The fact that you are considering a journey down the Romance Highway means that you want that, too. Technology can't stand in the way of the human connection if two people are seeking it.

Another thing that has not changed is the vulnerability you have to find in yourself in order to find a long-term partner. Having a deep and meaningful relationship means opening yourself up, being vulnerable, and showing a softer side. And probably most important, you have to be honest with yourself about where you are today and what your lifestyle is. Doing so will help you attract someone who fits that lifestyle—and makes it even better.

---

[1] *Aaron Smith and Monica Anderson, "5 facts about online dating," Pew Research Center FactTank, April 20, 2015, http://www.pewresearch.org/fact-tank/2015/04/20/5-facts-about-online-dating/.*

[2] *Rori Raye, "Two Steps to Being Irresistibly Confident," Dating Tips, eH Advice (a blog on eHarmony.com), http://www.eharmony.com/dating-advice/dating/two-steps-to-being-irresistibly-confident/#.VYolsUZd_VG.*

3 online dating: what it is and how to get good at it

I hear so many myths about online dating in my work: "The type of guy I like is not on online dating sites," "I'll look desperate," "I'm the CEO of a company and my reputation will be ruined." There are many ways to convince yourself that online dating isn't right for you. I'm going to try to convince you that it is.

First, some data, and then I'll get to the myths. The Pew Research Center survey that I mentioned earlier offers some pretty convincing statistics. For instance, 79 percent of people who use online dating sites said that online dating is a good way to meet people, while 70 percent responded that the wide range of potential dates means better chances for a romantic match. Additionally, the numbers show that individuals in the upper income brackets are very familiar with online dating: 57 percent of respondents with an annual household income of $75,000 or more know someone who uses online dating, and 40 percent know someone who met their spouse or partner online.[1]

Now, about those online-dating myths. The type of guy you like *is* on online dating sites. I have been researching this since 2008, and I can assure you that there are thousands of quality men your age populating these sites. Why do they go there? For the same reasons you will. They are successful, motivated, and intelligent, and they have experienced all the things we talked about in Chapter 2, including a shrinking pool of people in their social circles.

As for looking desperate? I'm not sure when being motivated and proactive became equated with desperation, but I want to dispel that notion right now. When you are out with a friend and see someone handsome, do you hide? I'm guessing not. There is no shame in desiring companionship, and none in meeting people at the electronic cocktail party, either.

If you are concerned about your professional reputation, there are ways to limit your visibility online and verify the legitimacy of people who express interest in you. Remember, desiring companionship is natural, and online dating has become accepted as the second most popular way to meet people (introductions via friends remains the first).[2]

In 2008 I was hired by a matchmaking firm to find men for the large number of women over fifty who were paying for its matchmaking services. These women felt that paying thousands of dollars to a matchmaker ensured that they would meet men in their income and social strata, since the men, too, would have invested a lot of money in these services and thus presumably would have a stake in a successful outcome. What I found when I looked in the database, however, was that there were several times as many women over fifty registered as men in the same age group. In fact, as I mentioned in the Introduction, many of the men hadn't even paid to join the service; they had been asked to let their names be added to the database by matchmakers who needed to meet their quota of introductions.

I decided to take a closer look at online dating to see how it compared to matchmaking services, and after researching the subject for two years, came to the conclusion that while matchmaking firms provided women a pond-sized number of quality men, online dating offered an ocean. In addition, the caliber of men I was finding online for clients was often higher than what was available using a match-maker. I came across many, many profiles of eligible men that my clients would never have a chance to meet using a matchmaker, but who I knew could be right for them. One client who ultimately met her partner online told me they had been shopping at the same grocery store for twenty years without ever crossing paths. A chance meeting in the bread aisle was no match for the power of online dating, which quickly brought them together.

how does online dating work?

In very basic terms, you sign up for a site, post a profile and pictures, and you're ready to start. I will discuss putting your best self forward with your photos and profile, but first I want to talk about the mechanics of how dating sites work. Some sites cost money, others are free. In my experience, the people who are most committed to online dating will use the paying sites; attaching a dollar amount to something, no matter how small, generates higher commitment. In addition, some sites offer more features and are thus more complicated than others (although if you find the features helpful, you probably won't find the sites that complicated).

While each site is slightly different and has attributes that might make it more or less appealing to use, here's what you can expect in general with online dating. There are many online dating sites, and different sites will appeal to different people for different reasons. To start with, think about signing up for one larger site as well as a smaller, niche site. Larger sites include Match.com (my favorite for its ease of use and the number of people on it), OKCupid.com, and eHarmony.com. Smaller and more specific sites, such as JDate.com, ChristianMingle.com, and RightStuffDating.com, tend to be targeted towards specific populations. Type "online dating sites" into a search engine and you will find many possibilities.

I want to emphasize that online dating is a methodical process. If you want success, you can't just throw a profile and some photos online and sit back and wait for someone to contact you. You need to take the wheel and drive this car straight onto the Romance Highway. Your goal is to discover men who are truly right for you where you are today. They are out there, but the only way you will find them is by actively perusing sites and then carefully vetting the profiles that come to your inbox.

Once you post a profile and photos, you can choose how visible you want to be. Again, this will vary with different sites, but you can be *visible*, meaning everyone on the site can see you; *private*, so that only men you email first can view your profile; or *hidden*, which means that no one can see you, even if you email someone. You can always change the setting down the road if you prefer to start out slowly. Once you've had a chance to see what the site is about, you can opt for a more public profile.

Log on and you will find your home page chock-full of information. You will have emails in your inbox from those interested in your profile, or, once you get going, people you are in communication with. Some sites send daily matches, profiles the site's algorithm determines might be suitable for you—

although, in my experience, the suggestions are usually not that great due to the algorithms' limited ability to match beyond basic preferences. There will also be lists of people who have viewed your profile, liked you, winked you, and "favorited" you (or whatever term each particular site uses). All of which gives you a starting point for profiles you can view if you are interested, based on the information available, which is limited to photos, ages, and locations.

I like to use the term *dating smart* when I talk about how to navigate dating in general, and online dating in particular. With online dating, dating smart includes ignoring the profiles you know right off the bat will not be right for you—someone twenty years younger, say, or a guy who lives two thousand miles away. As I said earlier, I recommend dating five years up or down, and unless you are willing to relocate or have a long-distance relationship, where someone lives should be near the top of the list in terms of importance. As for appearance, you can't help relying on photos when deciding whether or not to contact someone, but don't let a photo be the only criterion unless there is something in that person's appearance that you know you could never live with.

Some of the emails in your inbox will be from men who are obviously wrong for you. Beyond the obvious age or location issue, you might come across someone who starts a message with language like, "Hey, gorgeous" or "I'd love to take you out." The way people express themselves tells you a lot about them, and these are not people you'd likely be interested in getting to know. Ignore messages from men you can't imagine having a real conversation with, and delete their emails without even opening them. Online dating takes enough time without wasting it on inappropriate contacts.

On the other hand, if you get an email from someone just outside the recommended age range or who lives four hours away by car, but he writes a thoughtful email to you and appears serious, please do not ignore him. Common decency and good manners say you should respond with an equally thoughtful email saying, essentially, "Thank you for writing. I don't think we are a good match due to distance, but I appreciate your taking the time. I wish you the best of luck in your search." As with meeting someone in person, it takes courage to put yourself out there to someone; honor his effort and your own by being polite.

What about the email that comes in that looks promising? If the subject line looks interesting and the person is age- and location-appropriate, by all means open the email and see what he has to say. If everything looks good, enjoy the feeling of excitement and then open his profile. But here is something I cannot emphasize enough: read the ENTIRE profile. Most sites have very detailed profile forms, and if someone fills out the whole thing (which everyone should—be wary of those who have not), you can get a pretty good idea of who he is.

The mistake most women make is looking for a few superficial qualities and choosing or rejecting someone based on those. Things like photos, height, income, occupation, and kids. These are important, but they shouldn't be deal-breakers or deal-makers on their own. I can't tell you how many people I've worked with who have found long-term love with someone they would have initially rejected based on their predetermined standards for those criteria. Once they got to know the whole person, those "critical" attributes took a back seat to the more important ones that actually make a relationship work. Use a global lens when studying profiles, not a narrow one, and read all the way to the end of each one.

All online dating communications start out with email, but if someone sounds promising after a couple of emails, move the conversation to the phone. If a man only wants to communicate by email, he is probably cruising. A couple of emails in each direction should be enough; you don't want to email-date. If he's not willing to call after that, drop him and move on.

how to read digital body language: is he just cruising?

Even before you communicate with someone on an online dating site, you can ascertain a lot about the level of commitment someone is seeking by reading his profile.

Statements like "I want to develop things slowly," "I'm looking to meet people for friendship and fun," "I'm recently divorced and looking to meet people," and "I lead a very busy life and am very independent," as well as profiles that are self-absorbed and self-glorifying point to someone who, in my experience, tends to be selfish. If a man is looking for a woman ten or more years younger than he is, he is not being honest with where he is in his life and what will work, and that is a big red flag. You can also tell how serious someone is by how much time it appears he put into his profile. Those who are more serious about finding a partner tend to offer well developed, thoughtful profiles.

The length of a profile is also a good indicator. If it's five sentences, then they are not really committed to the process and finding someone long-term. On the other hand, if a profile length is starting to resemble *War and Peace,* the author is probably too self-absorbed. Ideally, a profile should be three or four paragraphs where every sentence does not begin with "I" (another indicator of self-absorption).

what to include (and avoid) in online dating emails

You're online and your profile and photos look great. Now what? Do you wait around to see if anyone notices? No! Remember, you are in charge here. Search for potential partners, and contact them. You will not appear desperate. This is how online dating works, and like most things in life, the good stuff comes to those who go after it!

Depending on your profile settings, you will either initiate all your contacts or receive some and initiate some. Once you find a man you'd like to contact, what do you say in that first email? Keep it simple and straightforward, friendly but not gushing. Here is the text I usually recommend: "Hi, I noticed your profile and wanted to reach out. We seem to have common interests (include them here to make sure they know you read their profile) and are looking for similar qualities in a partner. I would love to connect with you." You want to indicate that you noticed him and that you are interested, but you want to keep it basic for the first contact. Also, don't end your email with a question, as you don't want to get into an exchange that is predominantly question-based.

As I said earlier, after a couple of back-and-forth emails, give him your phone number and ask him to call. If he does, you are on the right path. Talking on the phone will humanize the whole process of online dating and move it closer to the "old-fashioned" way that you probably remember, before online dating even existed.

keys to success: great photos and profiles

The photos you post will give the first clues about who you are. You will be posting a few photos in addition to your cover picture, and you want to choose each of them carefully. Hire a professional photographer if you need to, but whether you use professional shots or ones taken by a friend, make sure they communicate the message you want to convey. Here are a few suggestions from an article on online dating from the *The Huffington Post*:[3]

Post a landscape shot
Landscape-oriented pictures are more likely to be clicked on than vertical or extremely close shots.

Don't crop someone out
Along with falling into that vertical no-no, cropping someone out of a photo generally results in less communication.

Don't snap from afar

Although you don't want too much of a close-up, you also don't want your picture to be taken from far away, which suggests you're hiding something about your appearance.

Don't feature shots of your buddy

Even if it's the most platonic of friendships, don't include a picture of yourself with another person, especially a member of the opposite sex. In general, keep pictures confined to shots of yourself.

Show happiness

Studies show that men prefer women who demonstrate happiness in their profile pictures, presumably because it's associated with femininity and nurturing.

Get outdoors

Taking a picture outside allows for the flattering effect of natural sunlight on skin. Just be careful to avoid squinting into the sun.

The cover photo should be similar to what you would look like on a first date. Aim for sophisticated, though that doesn't mean a little black dress and lots of jewelry. A glamour shot that is not your daily look is not the best representation of you. Find a compromise between tea at the Royal Palace and a sweaty post-hike look. Something that represents the true you, the way you generally look in person. Find an outfit that is flattering and a setting that is not distracting, and be the focus of the shot. Finally, the photo should be from within the last year; it needs to represent who you are today.

For the additional shots, four to six current photos are ideal. The first should be a glamour shot of you at your best, professionally photographed, if possible. A full body shot in special-occasion attire helps a man visualize what you'd look like on a date, at a party, or at a business function. A casual, fun shot and a picture of you with several friends or family can indicate your social circle and reveal your lighter side. Activity shots (e.g., yoga, tennis, water sports) show off your fun, athletic side. Potential partners want to know you will have time to spend with them and that your interests are versatile. So show that you know how to let your hair down after a long work week! Finally, if appropriate, include a corporate shot.

The profile you post will also tell a lot about you. If someone likes your photos and goes on to click on your profile, you want to continue impressing him there. Fill out as much of the information as you can; the personal details the sites ask for are an important part of expressing who you are. In addition, write two to four well-written, compelling paragraphs.

Start by asking friends for ten adjectives that best describe you. Next, check out other singles' dating profiles for inspiration. Then get to work! Showcase your diverse interests and incorporate both fun and sophisticated aspects of yourself, particularly in the travel and vacation sections. Balance writing about work with information about your values, hobbies, and social activities. Illustrate what you bring to a relationship as well as what you are seeking.

You want to excite people and stand out from the crowd, so share your passions. Your goal here is to discover common ground. For example: "I've never golfed before but I'm a great athlete and would love to play (particularly with a partner)," or "I'm very active and pick things up fast, so I want to learn to ski." Such statements show potential partners that you are receptive to new things and are willing to introduce them to new experiences as well.

If you don't feel you write well or you just want to know how what you've written looks to someone else, show it to a few trusted friends and incorporate their feedback. As with your photos, you want to project the air of someone who is happy, grounded, and open to new things.

what are the risks?

To a certain degree you are operating in the unknown when you go online, but employing smart strategies from the outset can help you avoid pitfalls. Some people do misrepresent themselves on their profiles, but in all the years I have been coaching people using online dating, I have yet to have a client come across a married man, one who has been in jail, or someone who might otherwise be dangerous.

The key is to become as familiar with someone as possible before you meet him. Start by looking for clues in their profile. Earlier in this chapter I talked about some characteristics of serious profiles versus ones written by men who are just playing. When you pursue a profile that looks interesting, don't set up a meeting until after you have spoken on the phone. In your phone conversation, you can ask questions about elements of their profile that you found interesting. "I see you like to travel in Europe. What are some of your favorite destinations?" "I see that you have two kids. Do they live with you?"

In addition, research potential dates on the Internet. Anyone who is a professional will have an online presence. You should be able to find enough information to verify what they are putting in their online dating profile.

Very few things in life are totally risk-free, but as we get older we learn how to minimize risks and how to move forward in spite of them. As always, listen to your inner voice. There are lots of men out there; you don't have to meet anyone who doesn't feel right to you.

how to handle online dating if you are nervous about it

As I've said before, you are in charge of your online dating experience. There is no need to move any faster than you are ready to move. You can choose whether to actively seek out other profiles, or, initially, just wait to see who contacts you (although ultimately, you need to get looking yourself). As you get used to how online dating works and start to meet interesting people, you can always pick up the pace. Give yourself three to six months to get familiar with the process and meet new people.

Remember that you *never* have to answer any person who does not feel right for you. If anything feels off, don't respond and delete the contact. If you do want to continue the conversation with someone or even meet them, remember a few basic things to keep it manageable:

- Set a goal for yourself of just meeting a couple of guys for the first month.

- Try to avoid getting into long email exchanges. Remember, give a man you are interested in your phone number, and have him call you.

- Get to know him on the phone first, and take your time before you decide to meet. If it doesn't feel right on the phone, don't go out with him.

- If you do decide to go out, remember the new rules for first dates, and start by giving yourself about one hour with him. Schedule a meeting at a small café or a nice place for a glass of wine, or take a walk. Know in your mind that it will be an hour and let him know that you have plans afterwards.

- If you are both interested in seeing each other again, it will happen. You don't have to figure everything out the first time you meet.

what can you expect in terms of results?

Your results will reflect the amount of energy you put into online dating. Don't be afraid to start out slowly, but keep your expectations realistic in relation to the effort you are putting into it. If you post a fabulous profile and photos, you will get noticed. Each online dating community has tips on how to get pushed to the top in search results, so make use of them as a means of upping your response rate.

After a few months, if you notice that traffic has started to slow to your profile, alternate your photos, rewrite parts of your profile or add to what is there, and reconsider the sites you are part of. You can even pursue listings in other cities if you travel regularly or are open to long-distance relationships. Nothing is set in stone with online dating; change things up to keep men visiting your page.

how to deal with burnout

Online dating isn't perfect and it can take time to find the right person—just like offline dating. Too-high expectations, however, can result in burnout, and many people find that after a few months of online dating they're ready to give it up. Unfortunately, that puts them right back where they were before they started, with few alternatives for meeting new people. In addition, frustration shifts your mindset, and that will be reflected in your communications and dates.

So, what do you do if burnout sets in? Below are a few suggestions from relationship expert Dr. Christie Hartman.[4]

Adjust your expectations
Most online dating burnout stems from unrealistic expectations, and most people go in expecting more

than online dating can deliver. People don't always turn out like their profiles and match-based online dating sites don't always pair you with perfect people. Instead, know what to expect, lower your expectations, and treat online dating like an adventure. You'll enjoy the process much more.

Change your criteria

It's hard to meet people when you have restrictive criteria. Remember, with online dating, preferences become requirements. You may prefer tall men, but if you specify you only want men over six feet tall, you effectively eliminate 85 percent of your pool. You may prefer men with master's degrees, but if you require it, you've ruled out a lot of smart, successful men. Keep your criteria broad, and see what comes your way.

Switch sites

Every online dating site offers something a little different. However, no matter how good an online dating site is, if you've been on it long enough (over a year), you've probably exhausted many of your options and must wait for new subscribers to show up. Most people only belong to one or two sites, so it can't hurt to try a new site and check out a new pool of options.

Take a break

If you need to, take an online-dating vacation. After a string of bad dates, bad emails, or other bad experiences, it's okay to hide your profile and ignore the site for a few weeks. Or, if your online dating burnout is more severe, feel free to let your subscription lapse. Spend some time with friends or try offline dating for a while.

time to get started

Online dating will open up a world of fun possibilities for you when it comes to meeting men who are right for you where you are today, and the best way to find out is to do it. Set realistic goals and expectations for yourself, based on where you are and how much effort you want to put into it at the beginning.

I often compare dating to a second job: it takes time and energy to do it well and have amazing results. And, as with anything new, you need to open up space for it in your life. If you are willing to start by opening up at least a little time and space for online dating, you will get a sense for what it is about, and early successes will likely give you even more energy to continue. I've seen it happen with so many of my clients who were initially skeptical. Now it's your turn!

[1] Aaron Smith and Maeve Duggan, "Online Dating and Relationships," Pew Research Center, October 21, 2013, http://www.pewinternet.org/2013/10/21/online-dating-relationships/.

[2] Larry Alton, "Online Dating Now Second Most Popular Way to Meet Someone," Social Media Week, February 4, 2014, http://socialmediaweek.org/blog/2014/02/online-dating-now-second-popular-way-meet-someone/.

[3] "Online Dating Picture: The Ideal Snap to Add to Your Online Profile," The Huffington Post, January 7, 2014, http://www.huffingtonpost.ca/2014/01/07/online-dating-picture_n_4556291.html.

[4] Dr. Christie Hartman, "How to Handle Online Dating Burnout," YourTango, http://www.yourtango.com/experts/dr-christie-hartman/how-handle-online-dating-burnout.

4 dating, from start to serious

after you've placed yourself in the dating world again, made the changes you needed to answer "yes" to the question of whether or not you would date yourself, and posted a fantastic profile and photos on online dating sites, it's time to start thinking about actually going out on dates. Hooray! The ideas in this chapter should help you to look forward to dates and enjoy the (fun) process of getting to know many great men.

One of the first things I tell clients—and one of the strategies I work closely with them on—is never to slot dates into small bits of time you have left over between all the other activities in your life. You want to schedule dates for when you are relaxed—not rushing off to an appointment or running in from a class—so you can focus on the person you are meeting. You know when someone is distracted, and he'll know if you are. Give yourself and him the gift of your full attention.

My client Cindy has a stressful job in sales in the high-tech industry and is very efficient with her scheduling. When she started dating, she looked for any small bits of time in her schedule to slot in dates. After work was one of those bits of time. One day she was running late from work and arrived at a first date both late and flustered. A look at her schedule that week should have been a red flag: her CEO was in town, she had meetings all week and a presentation on Friday, and she commuted forty miles between the Silicon Valley and San Francisco, where she lived. She scheduled the date on Wednesday evening of that week, and between a meeting running late and the rush-hour commute back to the city, she arrived at the restaurant twenty minutes late. She was stressed, had not shifted gears mentally from work, and didn't know how to get back on track during the date. Although the man seemed nice enough, her late arrival on the first date gave the message that he wasn't important enough to show up on time for. After suffering through several more dates with similar outcomes, it was clear something needed to change. She and I talked about her lifestyle, her schedule, and where she could find time that was unhurried and truly open.

Once she started looking closely at these things, she made a point of scheduling a few dates during times she had set aside as free in her calendar. This worked so well for her—she found herself actually enjoying the dates—that she decided to hold off on a get-together with a particular man she was interested in, as she was about to leave on a trip. Even though she knew he might find someone else while she was gone, she also knew that meeting him under hurried circumstances was setting herself up for failure.

Making dates, especially first dates, a priority in your schedule is critical if you are serious about finding a partner. Your mindset going into the date will be reflected in the outcome. If you are just fitting in a date because you have a little open air in your calendar, the date will reflect that lack of priority. Scheduling a date when you know you have the time and peace of mind to pay attention to the other person will allow you to put your true self forward and give you both a chance to see if a second date is in the cards.

Before you start planning dates, look at your overall schedule with a critical eye. I first talked about this in Chapter 2 in the context of finding someone whose lifestyle works with yours. Now you are looking at your schedule with an eye towards when you can realistically enjoy a date. When are you busy? When do you have time to relax? Are you freer during the week or on weekends? What are you doing on the days when you have more free time? Look at the answers to these questions closely, and then come up with the best time for you to schedule dates. Don't feel like you should be available all the time. It's not realistic. If you are only really free on weekends, don't schedule dates during the week. You will appreciate the ability to relax and enjoy your dates, and the men you meet will appreciate that you bring your true self when you meet them. There is a real power in owning your availability.

nerves and anxiety before the first date

When we want something, it's normal to feel anxiety about whether we will get it or not. Dating is no different. Almost everyone gets an attack of nerves when it comes to meeting someone for the first time, especially if there are high hopes and expectations. Keep in mind, however, that the key to handling nerves lies within you, not somewhere outside. Therefore, ignore the impulse to unwind by having a cocktail *before* the date; instead, give yourself a confidence-booster by following these ten steps, which come courtesy of psychotherapist Rachel Dack (with a little input from me).[1]

Pump yourself up, pre-date

Put on some music that makes you feel good, wear something that you feel attractive in, and focus on the parts of you that you feel most confident about. Come up with at least two positive qualities about yourself and let them soak in.

Avoid labeling anxious thoughts, feelings and sensations as bad

Anxious thoughts breed even more anxious thoughts, so break the cycle by taking a step back, reminding yourself that your anxiety will pass, and replacing negative thoughts with something positive. Try affirmations such as, "This will be fun," "I could meet someone great," or "I might make a new friend." Also remember that you can minimize your stress by doing advance research on your date by checking Google, Facebook, LinkedIn, and other sites.

Savor the possibility of finding love

Ask yourself what positive outcomes you can imagine from the date. Focus on hope, new potential, happiness, connection, and adventure.

Exercise to release endorphins

Try a yoga class to rejuvenate yourself and calm your mind, or head out for a thirty-minute power walk.

Recall other anxiety-provoking events and how they turned out

Reflect on experiences that went well for you despite an initial case of nerves.

Remind yourself that a first date is one single event in your life

Realistically, a date is only a small amount of

your time. You will get through it, and maybe even enjoy it. Confidence is key!

Practice conquering fears and anxieties in your everyday life

Make an extra effort to say thank you to a stranger holding the door at a coffee shop, strike up a conversation with someone at the gym, or get involved in a new activity. These exercises naturally make you feel good about yourself.

Plan out several conversation starters for the date

Having a plan is helpful, so put some thought into the date in advance. What are you confident talking about? Which subjects are interesting to you? What can you teach your date? Whatever you do, avoid talking too much about your work or children. Both are easy topics to slip into, and a little bit is o.k., but you want to focus on other things that define you, or things that you both have in common. Remember also to bring up aspects of your date's profile that resonated with you.

Give yourself a reality check
While looking for the right partner, you are likely to experience good dates and bad dates, fun dates and boring dates, dates where you click and dates where you don't. Be sure to manage your expectations.

Ground yourself before leaving for your date
Focus on your breathing while telling yourself something calming, comforting, and kind.

prepping for a date after work

By the end of the work day, none of us feels our most attractive. But that doesn't mean we can't perk ourselves up with a little attention to our appearance. If you are going on a date after work, don't show up looking the same as you did when you walked out of a meeting with the leadership team at 4:30. Here are some hints to help you shine on your date after a nose-to-the-grindstone day.

Mentally clock out
Schedule at least thirty minutes post-work and pre-date for personal time. Find a quiet space

where you can wind down with calm music and deep breathing exercises. Envision a successful date.

Change your look

Twenty to thirty minutes is all it takes to transform your appearance. Changing out of corporate wear works wonders in switching your focus from the afternoon's conference call to date-night anticipation. No need to rush home to change, either. Cashmere dresses under blazers are suitable for the office, yet are still soft and feminine; alternately, pack an extra blouse and pull out statement jewelry to glam your look. Always keep a pair of fresh hose in your bag in case you get a run at work.

Stand tall

Date night is the perfect time to flaunt your favorite heels, the ones you'd never wear to the office. *The Huffington Post* cites a study from the journal *Evolution and Human Behavior*, which concludes that "both males and females judged high heels to be more attractive than flat shoes."[2] Many women, however, are uncomfortable in heels; as an alternative, wedges and platforms are attractive shoes that give height but keep you from bobbling through the evening.

Give your hair some love

Embrace simple solutions such as a classic bun or experiment with quick yet attractive styles. Extensions are a popular fix for executives who are short on time. Consult a stylist for help placing extensions and to see which color, length, shape, and care regimen are best for you.

Sparkle

While subtle works for the office, an evening out is an opportunity to elevate your makeup. Switch lipstick from work to play and make sure to apply it correctly. You can find expert tutorials online that show you how to quickly create smoky eyes or shape your brows; others address facial contouring, which can alleviate self-consciousness around fine lines or extra weight. Embrace something new like false eyelashes to brighten tired eyes after back-to-back meetings. Above all, people remember a confident smile, so give your lips, teeth, and breath some attention before you walk into the date.

Spritz a little scent
A memorable fragrance will keep you lingering in your date's mind long after you've parted for the evening. You can tuck a sample-size perfume into your bag before you leave home in the morning. A lighter scent is appropriate for work but opt for a heavier perfume in the evening.

Polish your presentation
When we look our best, we act our best. Men tune into details such as hair, lipstick, accessories, confidence, smile, energy, and hands. Women often neglect their nails even though it's easy to travel with polish in your purse or invest in a gel manicure that can last for weeks with the right care.

Add (the right) color
Wardrobe color can affect how you are perceived. Find colors that work well for you, and invest in them.

Above all, wear your best attitude! A positive attitude is key to securing future dates. Forget about the office while you're on your date. Instead, focus on who you are, what you want to portray, and what you want to achieve.

master first dates

I have watched hundreds of clients go on first dates, and while some are great and some are not, there are definitely things you can do to prepare that give you a much higher chance of success. Here are my suggestions for mastering first dates.

Set yourself up for success
In addition to shooing away negative thoughts and wearing attire that makes you feel like a star, a great way to lift your confidence before a date is to practice two-minute power poses before you leave the house. Check out Amy Cuddy's 2012 TED Talk (https://www.ted.com/speakers/amy_cuddy), in which the social psychologist and Harvard Business School professor argues that not only

does body language affect how others see us, it can also change the way we view ourselves. In her Talk, Cuddy illustrates five different high-power stances that raise your confidence (she also demonstrates low-power poses, which many women subconsciously adopt on a regular basis). The "Wonder Woman" pose, for example, calls for placing your hands on your hips and standing with your legs elbow-width apart. For "Tall and Proud," bring your legs together, lift your chin and raise your arms into a V-shape.[3] As you practice the poses, work to ignore any feelings that you look ridiculous. Cuddy's presentation ranks No. 2 among most viewed TED Talks of all time and her techniques have been adapted throughout the business world. Clearly she's on to something!

Be present

You never know where a meeting may lead, romantically or otherwise. So make pleasant conversation and get to know your date. Learn! Your date's life will be rich with experiences and points of view.

Know your exit strategy

Prolonging unhappy early dates can have a negative impact on your energy and dating mindset. If it's not feeling right, finish your drink, express your thanks, and depart. If asked about a second date, remain noncommittal and offer to check your schedule and reconnect later. On a first date, everyone is nervous so try to give people the benefit of the doubt. At the same time, take care of yourself first and be mindful of your own well-being.

nerves and anxiety on the first date

Once on the first date, you might feel some (more) anxiety set in, but don't let it get in the way. Here are some tips from Rachel Dack for dealing with first-date jitters (these work on second and third dates, too).[4]

Remind yourself that you are conquering fears and anxieties

Despite pre-date urges to avoid dating altogether or cancel, you went on the date anyway. View this as an accomplishment and another example of how you refuse to let anxiety get in the way of what you want.

Maintain an attitude of curiosity and openness
Focus on learning about your date by listening attentively and asking questions. Being curious makes new experiences more exciting and rewarding while liberating you from anxious thoughts.

Make humor your friend
Humor is an ideal way to cut through an anxious moment or an awkward silence. Laughter is an instant mood booster, which is especially helpful if your date is anxious, too.

Stay in the moment
Let assumptions, judgments, worries, and "what ifs" pass by. Engage in what is happening then and there. Focus on what your date is saying and how you feel about it versus what is going on in your mind.

When you feel anxious, bring yourself back to the date
If you feel yourself becoming anxious, take at

least three breaths and think to yourself: "I can handle this and get through the date" or "I am conquering anxiety in this moment."

Let go of any need to be perfect
Striving for perfection is commonly linked with anxiety. Perfection is an impossible goal. Bring yourself back to reality and set yourself up for success by aiming to be your best self despite any self-defeating thoughts.

second dates and beyond

It takes two to tango and to make a second date happen. Sometimes dates seem to go well but the air-space afterwards is one big vacuum. Other times it's obvious that a second date will happen—or won't. The many factors that go into compatibility in any relationship show up in dating, too, and as you know, it's complicated. Here are some factors that go into deciding whether or not to move on to a second date.[5]

Chemistry
Both physical and mental, we can't deny the power of attraction.

Realness

People want a date who is genuinely interested in *them*—what they have to say and their interests. They want someone who is present and opens up about herself without an agenda. The first date should not be a place to tick off the list of future-spouse attributes.

Spontaneity

For some people, a willingness to be open and spontaneous is a huge factor in wanting to see the other person again.

Politeness

This shouldn't be surprising, but people really do prefer it when their dates are polite, and not rude or arrogant. This extends to how their date talks about others, from wait staff to other people in the café to their closest friends and family.

That "right" feeling

Sometimes that "right" feeling is just there and it's inexplicable. That's all I can say about that!

First dates are not always fireworks and string music, but just because they can be on the boring side does not mean someone is not for you. A boring first date might indicate a lack of drama in the future; sometimes quiet people turn out to be deeper, more committed, more intelligent, and ultimately more interesting than the men who sweep you off your feet in the first meeting. I'm not saying a boring first date is a guarantee of future happiness, but don't write it off right away. Try a second date and learn more about him.

I advise my clients to always date more than one person, if possible, for the first six weeks of any relationship that looks promising. Don't focus on one man too quickly, even if he seems like he could be "The One." Keep dating so you always have something to compare to before you decide to exclusively date just one person.

For a second date, I recommend breakfast, brunch, lunch, or dinner. If you like each other enough to see one another again, schedule a longer date during the day, like a museum trip, a hike, or a bike ride. Build up to spending more time together when you know you both want that time. Don't, however, schedule a long outing for your second date.

After three or four dates, I recommend you avoid texting and instead use the phone when you want to communicate. As I said earlier, if he is not willing to talk on the phone, he is showing that he doesn't understand the importance of connection. Or he is lazy. You both need to make the effort to connect. At least a couple times a week between dates, call each other. Talking will help develop your emotional connection.

Whatever happens on first dates, don't feel stressed if they clearly won't turn into second ones. Compatibility is a complex thing, and there will be more men who are not compatible than who are, or we'd all be happily paired up by now. Feel proud of yourself and stand tall—you are getting out there and dating, and that's what's important. The more you do it, the more you will find men you want to see on a second date—and beyond.

chemistry vs. compatibility

Here is an age-old question: what's more important in a relationship, chemistry or compatibility? Is it more important that you share interests, or that you can't get enough of your attraction for each other?

There is not one right answer for everybody, but it's an important question to ask yourself. Perhaps the man you are dating is attractive and romantic, but does it matter that he will never want to go to your favorite movies with you? Or maybe you have found someone who likes so many of the same things you do that you could go on dates for years and never run out of mutually interesting activities, but when it comes to attraction and romance, there's not much there. Which is better?

Maybe neither. Maybe one or the other. Or maybe you need to find someone more in the middle, someone you are attracted to who also shares a significant number of interests with you. Again, there is no right or wrong answer. You don't have to decide this on the first or second date, but you don't want to go too far down the Romance Highway with someone if there is a significant gap in either chemistry or compatibility.

physical intimacy

I am a huge advocate for going slowly with physical intimacy. In my experience, women feel a much deeper emotional connection to men once the relationship gets intimate, which can make them vulnerable to getting hurt. It's important to communicate about what you want, what he wants, and where the relationship is going. The exact timing for intimacy will be different for everyone, but I recommend having longer dates and asking deeper questions before you get intimate. You want to find out what happened in his past relationships, see him in different situations, and get to know who he really is. You want to know him and really like him before you take the big step of being physically intimate.

Everyone has their negotiables and non-negotiables in a relationship. I recommend that you make sure that whatever is critical to you in a relationship is there before you get intimate with someone. He will not change who he is just because your relationship goes to the next level. In fact, physical intimacy makes the challenging aspects of a relationship harder to deal with, because while you might have taken yourself to a higher level of commitment, he might not have. Dating smart means knowing when the time is right for you. Intimacy is a wonderful and important part of a relationship, but only when you know that he is as interested as you are, and you feel that he is meeting your other relationship needs, as well.

body language: what are you trying to say vs. what you are really saying

You might remember flirting and using body language when you were dating in your twenties. It seemed natural and easy then, but what about now? Believe it or not, body language is important no matter what age we are, and by the time we're older, chances are we've learned to read the signals more clearly. So how do you say what you want with age-appropriate body language?

In an article in *The Huffington Post*, Anthonia Akitunde, who writes extensively about women, talks about body language in older women, specifically addressing the negative signals women can give off.[6]

First on the list is wearing too many clothes. When we feel self-conscious about our arms or our legs or our neck we tend to cover up completely. But that sends a subconscious message that we don't find ourselves attractive, a message that creates a barrier and turns men away. When you dress for a date, show some skin but don't go overboard—just enough to show that you are confident in your age and your body.

Poor eye contact is also a turn-off for men. It's hard to maintain eye contact, but with practice you can get better at it. Try it in small doses with men you meet during your day. A little bit at a time is fine as you say hello or pass someone, but you will find it gets easier to hold eye contact for longer the more you do it. A fear of rejection is normal, but most people will be delighted when you make eye contact, and are not likely to turn away (and if they do, it's probably more from their own fears).

You can create physical barriers with your body, as well. Crossed arms or leaning away from your date send clear messages. If you are interested in each other, however, look down; you're likely to find that your feet are pointed toward one another, rather than angled in different directions. Another big signal is how you cross your legs. If your date is on your left and you cross your left leg over your right, you create a distance and a barrier. Crossing your right over your left, on the other hand, turns you naturally in his direction and creates a shared space.

You can also use objects to throw up an emotional wall. Anything from your coffee cup to your wine glass to a menu in front of your face can feel like a safety net, but sends the message that you are protecting yourself from your date in some way.

Don't worry so much about your body language that you become anxious or tense on your dates, but just be aware of the subtle messages you can send, and sync them with the ones you really want to send. And if you don't get it all right the first time, don't worry. Life is about practicing, and dating will give you plenty of that.

the friend setup

Perhaps one of the most awkward situations in dating is when well-meaning friends want to set you up with someone they know. Like I said, your friends are well-meaning, but chances are they are not paying close attention to what sort of person you really need or want, or how compatible you are likely to be with one of their friends who just happens to be single.

It's almost inevitable that the friend setup will happen to you at least once, so I want to address some ways that you can deal with it and avoid a situation that is clearly wrong.

If a friend calls and says she wants to set you up with someone she knows, don't jump right in with, "That's great! Thanks!" Take an emotional step back, thank her for thinking of you, and tell her you're interested but first would like to know more. What can she tell you about him? What is he like? Ask the questions you would want to know the answers to if you were checking for compatibility on an online dating site. Ask whatever you need to know to be convinced that her enthusiasm could indeed result in an interesting outcome. If your friend does not have immediate answers to your questions, request that she find out more. It's possible she knows little about the man beyond his single status, which is not enough of a criterion to go on.

If you do decide to go on the date, think about it as an opportunity to meet someone who will help you expand your network, rather than thinking of the man as possibly being "The One." Sometimes friends do get it right, but in my experience, that's not terribly common. Either way, just remember: they do mean well.

[1] Rachel Dack, "Ten Ways to Tame First Date Anxiety," eHarmony, http://www.eharmony.com/dating-advice/dating-tips/ten-ways-to-tame-first-date-anxiety/#.VdIUKvknrYC.

[2] Dr. Raj Persaud and Adrian Furnham, "Why Do High Heels Make Women More Attractive?" The Huffington Post, August 1, 2013, http://www.huffingtonpost.com/dr-raj-persaud/why-do-high-heels_b_3691829.html.

[3] "Fake it 'til you become it: Amy Cuddy's power poses, visualized," TEDBlog, December 13, 2013, http://blog.ted.com/fake-it-til-you-become-it-amy-cuddys-power-poses-visualized/.

[4] Rachel Dack, "When Anxiety Strikes during Your Date: Six Ways to Manage It," eH Advice (a blog on eHarmony.com), http://www.eharmony.com/dating-advice/dating-advice-for-you/when-anxiety-strikes-during-your-date-six-ways-to-manage/#.VdImBPknrYA.

[5] Laura Schaefer, "Should You Go on a Second Date?" Happen (a blog on match.com), http://www.match.com/cp.aspx?cpp=/cppp/magazine/article0.html&articleid=13230.

[6] Anthonia Akitunde, "Body Language is Still Important in Dating over 50," The Huffington Post, June 26, 2013, http://www.huffingtonpost.com/2013/06/25/body-language-dating-over-50_n_3423304.html.

XX

5 dating skills mastery: advanced rules for the road

n̈

now that you have laid the groundwork for a successful journey on the Romance Highway, it's time to master a few skills that will help immeasurably as you begin to meet men. As I've said, dating is almost like a full-time job, and just as you want to bring your best self to work and minimize mistakes (though don't forget to see them as learning opportunities when you make them!), you want to do the same with dating. Also, it is important to take good care of yourself and maintain a good mindset while dating—not to mention in life in general. Keeping these things in mind, here are a few advanced relationship tips on topics ranging from staying optimistic to awakening your warrior-woman self.

optimism and resilience: maintaining your marathon mindset

If you have been divorced or widowed, you have experienced a great loss already, and you have survived. But much of how you move forward will be determined by what you focus on. If the loss is what you think about the most, you are likely to be more fearful and cautious and even stuck when it comes to entering the dating world. If the fact that you have survived and in fact might even be in a better place now takes precedence in your thoughts, you have a good dose of optimism already at work.

Optimism is important in the dating world because things generally do not progress in a linear way. You will meet men who are not interesting to you or are not interested in you; you will sometimes go for long periods between meeting men; you will meet someone interesting and date for a while, but ultimately it won't work out. All of these situations are normal, and none of them indicate that you will never meet the right person. They will be interspersed with times where you meet many interesting men, go out on fun dates, get lots of positive feedback, and, with effort and luck, eventually meet someone for the long-term. Regardless of how things happen on your romance journey, you have to stay optimistic and resilient.

Emily Esfahani Smith, who writes about psychology and relationships, states it succinctly in *The Atlantic*, "[H]aving a positive outlook in difficult circumstances is not only an important predictor of resilience—how quickly people recover from adversity—but it is *the* most important predictor of it."[1]

Here are ten ways to maintain a positive attitude—towards yourself, towards dating, and towards life. The first three come from relationship columnist and blogger Christine Coppa, who talks about ways to improve your attitude towards dating in a post for YourTango.[2]

Look the part
Maybe red lipstick makes you feel sexy. New shoes could be your secret weapon. When you look good, you feel good. Positive emotions make you feel better, and when you feel better, you attract good things.

Stop lying to yourself
If you want a boyfriend (or husband), admit it. Tell the universe what you want and it will come to you.

Go to your happy place
What place gets you out of a funk? Your happy place could also be his.

Further ideas on how to cultivate a positive attitude, courtesy of eHarmony:[3]

Don't let tomorrow spoil today
You don't know what will happen tomorrow. Don't let it steal your happiness in the present moment.

Afirm yourself and others, often
You'll all feel better about yourselves!

Pay attention to your thoughts
Steer internal messages toward hopeful, positive expectations.

Smile and be mindful of what you say
Adjusting your facial expression causes a physiological change: you to begin to feel the

emotion you are showing. Words d
keep them positive.

Play!
Schedule time for recreation and fun, just as you
do for work.

Set a goal and go for it
A small goal or a big one, accomplishing it will
lift your spirits.

Remember these wise words
"A pessimist sees the difficulty in every
opportunity; an optimist sees the opportunity
in every difficulty." (Sometimes attributed to
Winston Churchill)

In addition, don't forget Tony Robbins' transformational vocabulary from Chapter 1 and the power poses
discussed in Chapter 4. All of these techniques will
keep you thinking and feeling positively for the long
haul!

detours and setbacks: how to reset

As I've said before, a journey down the Romance
Highway is not linear. You take detours, intentionally

or not, and you reach roadblocks. You might meet a man you think is wonderful and he suddenly goes radio silent. Someone else promising reveals that he isn't interested in Ms. Right, but just wants Ms. Right-For-Now. Or maybe you don't meet anyone you even remotely like for some time. You can end up feeling like you are stranded at Disappointment Central. Below are tips for quickly getting back on track.

Go from victim to victor mentality

Regardless of what has happened, take control of how you feel about it and how you work through it. Start with five long, slow, deep breaths. This will physiologically change you, help you to reset, and give you an expanded sense of time and relaxation.

De-escalate your reactions

Avoid the tendency to blow things out of proportion. Was it just one bad date, or even two? If it was more, think about what you can take away from those experiences and use that information going forward. Put it all in the context of your overall life. Take anything you've learned and make it a positive—this newfound knowledge will help you become your best dating self.

navigating discussions: past relationships

As you get to know men you are interested in, the topic of past relationships will invariably come up. Save those conversations for when you are on a more solid footing with a man, and make sure you've worked through your emotions enough that you can talk about past relationships without seeming bitter, vindictive, or so stuck on your ex that your date just wants to pay the bill and get out of there. Forever. You want to be able to talk about exes as factually as you can, and as quickly as you can; no dwelling on long, drawn-out situations from the past. You need to live in the present and show that you are doing so.

In the same vein, don't talk about any previous marriages too much up front. Depending on your feelings, including any residual ones you have not dealt with (but please, do deal with them before you start dating), you might come across as a bitter and angry person, when you normally would not be that way. Work through any lingering issues about your divorce, and then start meeting people in the here and now.

navigating discussions: finances

Nobody likes to talk about money, and in the context of relationships, it gets even more complicated. Women are often financially secure once they reach fifty, and are understandably protective of their money. Financial self-sufficiency is another element of self-esteem. It is natural not to want to be with a man who isn't as secure as you are economically. The question of dating someone older also brings up the issue of becoming a caretaker if and when your partner's health declines—potentially making you a nurse with a purse. Wherever you are financially, know that you do not have to enter the dating world with the intent of marrying, if the question of finances is a sticky one for you. You can commit to a relationship without getting married, assuming the man feels the same way. Whatever you decide, at some point you will have to enter into a discussion of finances and how to handle them. Remember that it's probably an emotional topic for both of you, so try to keep the discussion respectful and open.

communication that works

It's not really the topics of discussions that cause problems—it's the way you and your partner approach those topics. You both need to find ways to talk so that the other will listen. Robert Leahy, Ph.D., director of the American Institute for Cognitive Therapy and a clinical professor of psychology at Weill-Cornell Medical School, offers the following ten techniques for getting beyond shouting and sulking so that you can find a way to communicate in a way that ensures everyone is heard.[4]

> ### Pick the right time
> Sometimes you think you need to be heard the minute you have a thought or feeling. But your partner might be wrapped up in something else at that moment, or just not in the right mood. If you start talking and he isn't listening, instead of getting angry and lashing out, calmly ask, "Is there a better time to talk?" And, if you are the

listener, play fair—give your partner a
reasonable alternative.

Edit it down

Once we start talking, it's easy to get carried
away. Try to limit your comments to clear, short
sentences. Pause, ask for feedback, and then wait
for your partner. One way of editing it down is
to set up a reasonable time period to spend on a
topic. For example, "Can we spend about ten
minutes talking about this?"

Make communication a two-way street

If you feel your partner hasn't really heard what
you are saying, then try asking, "Can you repeat
back what I said?" Or if you want your partner
to help you think of things differently, you might
say, "I wonder if I'm seeing things the right way
here." Or if you want problem-solving, you
might say, "I wonder what I can do to make it
work."

Don't catastrophize

Sometimes we think that the only way to be
heard is to make everything sound awful.
Instead, try to keep things in perspective, stick to

the facts, and work to keep things from unraveling. Keep your voice calm and don't get carried away. Use a softer tone and you will be heard more clearly.

Don't attack

Your listener is not likely to be a good audience if your discussion is a series of attacks and criticisms. This doesn't mean you can't get your point across and assert yourself. It simply means that you need to communicate in a way that is not hostile. Making suggestions for change while giving credit for positive responses will always get you more attention and cooperation than outright attacks.

Let your partner know if you want to solve problems or if you simply want to vent

My experience is that sometimes we just want to vent our feelings, to have our partner lend a sympathetic ear. That's okay, but your partner needs to know where you are going with it, especially if he has a tendency to try to "fix" everything, which can be frustrating when you're just looking for comfort. To avoid a misunderstanding, consider setting a time limit for your discussion—fifteen minutes or less for venting and sharing, and then either drop the topic or move on to problem-solving.

Listening is not agreeing

Listening is hearing, understanding, reflecting, and processing information. I can listen to your thoughts and feelings without agreeing with your point of view. You and I are different people. It doesn't mean I don't care for you if I don't agree with you. It means I am hearing you.

Respect advice

If you are turning to your partner for support, you are likely to get feedback—feedback that will probably include some advice. Maybe the advice is not helpful; maybe it's even irrational. But if you want to be heard, you have to be willing to respect the advice-giver. You don't have to like or take the advice. But you should always see advice and feedback as information. Take it or leave it, but respect it either way.

If you describe a problem, describe a solution

In some cases it can help move the discussion along if you offer solutions to the problem you are describing. Your solution doesn't have to be an *order* to do something. It can be tentative, reasonable, one of several possibilities.

Validate the validator

One of the most helpful things that you can do as a speaker is to support the person who is supporting you. Thank them for caring enough to listen to and support you.

children and "Brady Bunching" families

Many women worry about how to handle dating with children still living at home. Not only does this scenario require more careful scheduling of dates, but your children might not experience the excitement of a new man in your life in quite the same way that you do. One firm rule I have is not to bring a date home until you and he have developed a serious relationship that looks like it might go somewhere.

Having a revolving door of men coming into and going out of your kids' lives will upset them and introduce more instability than they might already be feeling. If a relationship is getting serious and you feel that you are both committed, then it is important for your partner to get to know your children, and vice versa. But until that time, keep your dating and your parenting lives separate.

If you have children at home, it is likely that you will end up finding someone at the same stage of life. What happens when things get serious? Do you combine families, or live parallel lives where you see each other but keep your families separate? It's fine to do the latter for a while, but if there is true commitment in your relationship, you are going to need to look at blending your families eventually. There is no rush. Take all the time you both need to build a strong foundation in your relationship, and address whatever concerns your children may have. No situation is perfect, but if you move slowly and consciously, you should be able to blend families successfully.

knowing when to walk away

While it can be hard to admit, it really is important to recognize when a relationship is not working. When you know what you and your partner really want (which means communication from both of you!) and you can discern whether those desires are compatible, it should be pretty clear whether you want to stay or go.

My friend Claire dated Thomas, a man she felt would become her husband, for two years. He was in his mid-forties and had never been married when they met, but said from the beginning of their relationship that he had always been interested in getting married and having children. After more than a year of dating, however, and with no proposal on the horizon, she began to question whether or not he still wanted those things—or even if he ever had. She was in her late thirties at the time, and very much hoped to have children, a fact she had made abundantly clear.

Claire loved Thomas and really felt he could be "The One," but his unwillingness or inability to commit was troubling. After many conversations with him (not to mention quite a few with herself and her friends), she realized that it was possible he would delay a definitive answer indefinitely. She didn't want to lose him, but she also *really* didn't want to lose the chance to find someone who shared her desire for marriage and a family. They attended couples therapy, but after a few months she realized she was going to need an unqualified answer, and gave him a deadline of six months. As the clock wound down on that deadline, however, he finally admitted he was not ready to get married and didn't know if he ever would be.

As painful as those words were, Claire knew that she finally had the clarity she had been asking for all along, and they broke up.

Almost a year later, Thomas, with whom she had had no contact, sent her a card, asking if she would consider dating him again. This time around, he promised, his goal was marriage.

It turned out that while they had been apart, he had decided to work on why he was so afraid of commitment. He knew he wanted to be with Claire, but he didn't know how to overcome his fear. After a lot of hard work in therapy over that year, Thomas grew to understand that he did, in fact, want to marry her, and launched an all-out effort to win her back.

After much thought, she agreed to give him a chance. In the end, they got married and had two children, and they just celebrated their ten-year anniversary. If Claire had not discovered her inner strength and conviction when she did, however, things might have turned out very differently.

But the other factor is that she really listened to what he was saying and took him at his word. When he said he didn't know if he would ever be ready for marriage—knowing it was something she really wanted—she knew it was time to fold her cards.

The issues in every relationship will be different. For Claire, it was marriage. For others it could be divergent interests, different values, disagreements about money or intimacy or children, or really almost anything. No matter what the issue, however, asking the questions and really listening to the answers should give you the information you need to move ahead, whatever the direction.

awakening your warrior-woman self

Becoming confident is one of the biggest and most important changes I see in women I work with. So many have been in relationships where they don't have a voice or a sense of their own self-worth, and when issues come up that matter to them, they feel powerless to get what they want.

The first thing you need to do is to admit to yourself that you matter in your relationships. All women do—and I work hard to instill that certainty in my clients until they believe it, too. Being a woman warrior does not mean carrying a spear and heading into battle. It means that you build an internal warrior who helps you express your feelings and desires in relationships, so that your voice is heard as clearly as everyone else's. Women who do that have no need for spears.

I have found in my work that so many of my clients have wonderful, clear, powerful voices when it comes to succeeding at work, raising their families, even taking care of themselves physically. But when it comes to their intimate relationships with men, they become another person: afraid to express their feelings, hesitant to stick up for themselves, and cautious about asking questions when they don't like something.

The message that women's voices don't count as much as men's still underlies many aspects of our culture. Men who speak up are considered strong, bold, and able to get what they want or need—and are applauded for it. Women who do the same are labeled difficult, whiny, high-maintenance, and dramatic. As a result, women are much less likely than men to ask for a raise at work. Men ask because they feel it is right. The outcome? On average, women are still paid almost 25 percent less than men for the same work. Despite an effort towards salary parity, especially among the younger generation, there is still an unspoken message that women should not make too much noise lest it prove unpleasant for the people around them.

Well, I'm here to say forget all that and find your voice! Remember the story from Chapter 2 about Teresa, who finally mustered the courage to ask the man she was dating if they could accommodate her schedule, not just his, and he told her he didn't see their relationship as long-term? As painful as that was for her to hear, she knew that she had done the right thing by voicing her needs. Given his attitude, the outcome of that relationship was inevitable, but once she knew where he stood, she didn't waste another minute with him.

Many women fear that if they speak up, the man will leave. Let him! Any relationship damaged by a woman standing up for the fact that she matters is not a relationship worth her time. If the needs and desires and dreams of both partners are not of equal importance, the relationship is too unbalanced.

Women who lack an inner warrior often feel they are being needy and possessive if they ask questions of their partners such as, "Why didn't you call when you said you would?" or "Why do you fit me in only when it's convenient for you?" or "Why aren't you doing anything special for me?" Society telling us we are irrational for wanting those things does nothing to help the cause.

The truth is that we all—men *and* women—have needs, and women's needs are as valid as men's. Any successful relationship has to meet both parties' desires. If it doesn't, it falls apart. We can't expect our partners to be mind-readers; we must tell them what we need and how we feel. Address problems before they get out of hand and while you are still able to do it calmly. Be a feminine warrior—leave the spear behind but show up with your sense of self-worth intact.

[1] Emily Esfahani Smith, "The Benefits of Optimism Are Real," The Atlantic, March 1, 2013, http://www.theatlantic.com/health/archive/2013/03/the-benefits-of-optimism-are-real/273306/.

[2] Christine M. Coppa, "Three Ways to Change Your Bad Dating Attitude," YourTango, http://www.yourtango.com/201058420/3-ways-change-your-bad-dating-attitude.

[3] Ashley, "15 Ways to Cultivate an Optimistic Outlook," eH Advice (a blog on eHarmony.com), http://www.eharmony.com/dating-advice/about-you/15-ways-to-cultivate-an-optimistic-outlook/#.VjfnyivcCy1.

[4] Robert Leahy, Ph.D., "Relationship Communication: How to Talk So That Your Partner Will Listen," The Huffington Post, February 8, 2011, http://www.huffingtonpost.com/robert-leahy-phd/relationship-communication_b_815699.html.

6 a personal note

Congratulations! The fact that you have gotten to this point in the book means that you are serious about pursuing this exciting new adventure in your life. You are probably hesitant about it, too, but that's perfectly natural. It's hard to start something new, especially something like dating where you have to put yourself out there and allow yourself to be open and vulnerable in ways you might not have had to be for some time. So, right now, pat yourself on the back and feel good that you have gone beyond just thinking about dating again to actually starting the process, because even opening yourself up to the information in this book is a big step.

I truly believe that everyone who really tries the steps outlined in this book will find someone who is right for them. But it's not just a matter of following the steps; it also has a lot to do with your outlook. Here are some essential points that I want to reiterate.

1. Remember to stay optimistic and to allow yourself to bounce back from disappointments and try again. Dating is like life—it's a mix of positive and negative, and your job is to enjoy the positive and be resilient when faced with the negative.

2. Whatever it takes for you to get to a point where you are truly open to meeting new people and the joy that they can bring to your life, do it before you start dating. Shed your fear and, especially, any bitterness about past experiences, so that you do not become bogged down with excess baggage on the Romance Highway.

3. Know yourself, or get to know yourself better, so that you know what you bring to relationships and what you need from them. That clarity will save you the time and effort involved in pursuing people who are not a good fit for your life.

4. Be methodical about the dating process. It might sound rigid, but it really makes a difference. The steps and hints in this book come from many years of watching women and men succeed in finding new love. They work!

5. Patience is a virtue in life *and* on the Romance Highway. Most things we really love and treasure in our lives did not come to us without time and effort. Which is part of the reason they are so valuable to us.

6. Trust yourself and your instincts, and listen to your inner voice. But also trust that there are wonderful people out there, that you will meet many of them as you move along on this journey, and that there is someone—probably more than one person— who is right for you.

One of the wonderful side benefits of embarking on this journey is that you will meet people who could very well become good friends even if you don't click romantically. Your social circle will grow, which opens up many possibilities for enjoyment in your life beyond your primary relationship. Becoming your own matchmaker is a way to open up your life to new experiences. What could be better than that?

As I mentioned in the Introduction, I have been in the matchmaking/relationship-coaching world for nearly thirty years. I think I can say I've almost seen it all, but one thing I have never seen on online dating sites is someone who is dangerous. Call me an optimist, but I have looked through thousands of profiles, talked to hundreds of men, and worked with scores of clients over the years, and never once have I come across someone I was concerned about. The Internet and social media sites are fantastic sources of information, and can help you research just about anybody. Use them!

I love what I do and can never get enough of watching people find new love, especially after loss. I am a firm believer in the need for human connection, and my conviction in the method I've outlined in this book grows out of seeing so many couples come together after working with me.

I know this will work for you, too.

Trust yourself to be your own matchmaker, and whatever else you do, have fun with it. I'll see you on the Highway!

XX

acknowledgments

books are the effort of so many people beyond just the authors, editors, and publishers, and this one would not be in your hands if it were not for the people I'm lucky enough to call my tribe.

My mother, Betty Zampa, was not only my first roadmap in life, but has also taught me so many lessons-by-example in her fifty-nine-years-and-counting marriage to my father. In addition, she gave me invaluable insights into her widowed and divorced friends, insights that helped shape me as a dating strategist working with this demographic.

Elizabeth Hitchcock, my business partner, and I met when she became my client many years ago. Since then, after finding love, she has become a friend, a mentor, and a priceless advisor to my business.

Without her this book would never have gotten out of first gear and my business would not be what it is today—or what it will be in the future. She has always believed in me and helped me put my best foot forward.

Danielle Machotka came into this project as a writer who knew nothing of what I do, or why and how I do it. She fully embraced my effort and dedication to helping my clients, absorbed my knowledge, and became my voice, allowing me to write this book.

The women and men—but for this book, particularly the women—who have hired me to ride with them on their trip down the Romance Highway have not only shown courage in picking up the phone to call, but have taught me more in my nearly thirty years in this business than I have learned anywhere else. So much of my work stems from their trust and belief in me and in this process.

No house can stand for long without a foundation. My wonderful husband, Mike, has been there every step of the way, providing stability and being my No. 1 cheerleader. I wouldn't be where or who I am without him.

Finally, last but absolutely not least, my three wonderful children, who are patient and supportive, and who always seem to understand when I have to get to work.

about the author

Cassie Zampa-Keim is a renowned dating and relationship strategist, author, speaker, workshop leader, and coach. She is the founder and CEO of Innovative Match, a national relationship-services firm, and author of the syndicated "Ask Cass" blog.

One of the industry's leading experts on dating after fifty, Cassie has created a new map for transforming her clients' dating lives, using decades of successful singles coaching, technological insight, intuition, and a compassionate heart.

Cassie began her career almost thirty years ago working at one of the nation's top matchmaking firms. She channeled her fierce innovative spirit and extensive personal network to quickly create a thriving national client base. Enthralled by technology's impact on the dating landscape, she was one of the early pioneers of using online dating with clients.

Cassie launched Innovative Match to incorporate her dating strategies with a personalized coaching approach, to better help clients in the prime of their lives ride the wave of a new dating world. She and her team develop a holistic view of each client to customize their experience, applying principles from Cassie's background as a certified life coach.

Recognized as one of the World's Top Dating Experts by Older Dating UK, Cassie holds a BA in communications and psychology and is a graduate of Harvard Business School's Executive Entrepreneurship Program. She also studied at Cambridge University in England.

www.innovative-match.com

Made in the USA
Monee, IL
21 June 2021